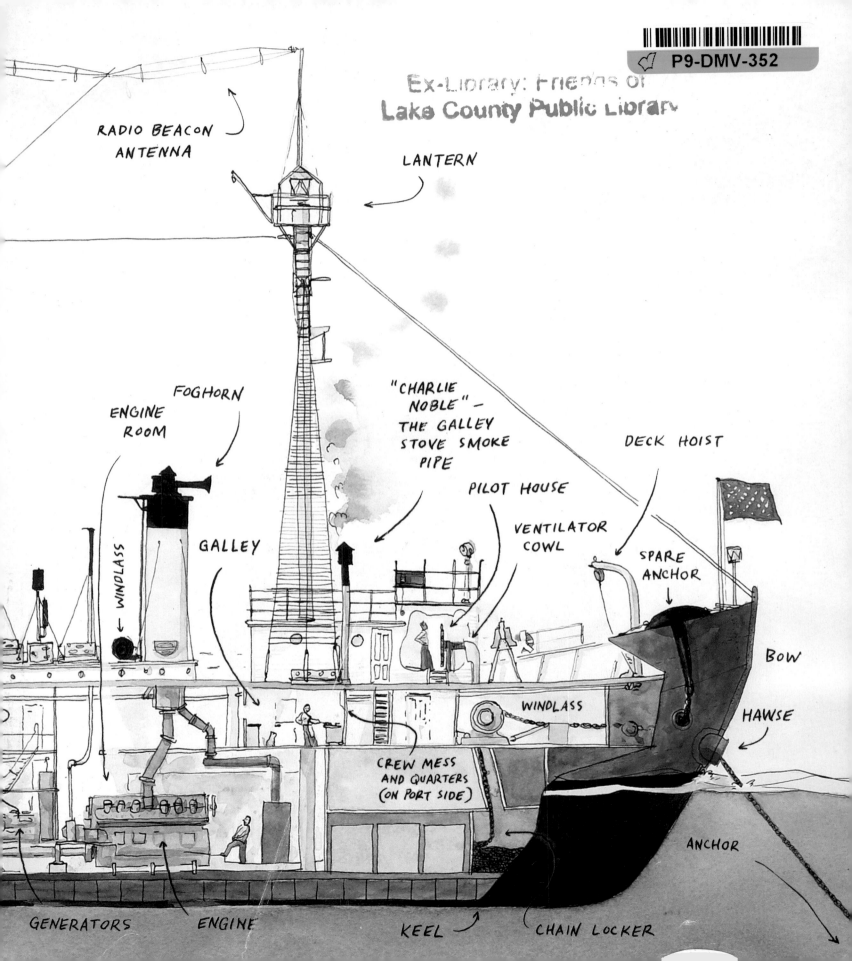

RADIO BEACON ANTENNA

LANTERN

FOGHORN

ENGINE ROOM

"CHARLIE NOBLE" — THE GALLEY STOVE SMOKE PIPE

DECK HOIST

GALLEY

PILOT HOUSE

VENTILATOR COWL

SPARE ANCHOR

WINDLASS

BOW

WINDLASS

HAWSE

CREW MESS AND QUARTERS (ON PORT SIDE)

GENERATORS

ENGINE

KEEL

CHAIN LOCKER

ANCHOR

LIGHTSHIP

for Natalie Greenfield

ACKNOWLEDGMENTS

The particular lightship crew members in these pages are fictional characters, but the routines, the work, and the dangers they experience were all very real parts of lightship service, and I have done my best to relate them accurately. (This effort extends to the depiction of the shipboard cat; whether allowed to or not, crews would in fact sometimes keep pets or mascots on board.)

I would like to thank the following individuals for appreciated help with this work. Jeff Remling, Curator of Collections and Director of Operations at the South Street Seaport Museum in New York City, answered questions and allowed me to nose around otherwise inaccessible corners of Light Vessel 87 when this book was just a notion. Paul Cora, Curator at the Baltimore Maritime Museum, opened hatch after hatch on LV 116 for me, explained obscure and dangerous-looking switches, and gave me access to the records of the ship's service and to many useful photographs. James Rutledge, who served on LV 118 at Cornfield Point off the coast of Connecticut, and Hal Washburn, who served on LV 115 at the Frying Pan Shoals off the coast of North Carolina, shared memories and photographs and generously answered questions. I am grateful to them all for helping to make this book more interesting and accurate than it otherwise could have been. Any remaining inaccuracies are my own.

Symbols like the one on the previous page were used on navigational charts to mark the position of lightships. They were accompanied by the name of the lightship station and by identifying information for the ranges and patterns of the ship's horn, light, and radio beacon signal. This information helped sailors know where to look for, and how to identify, a particular lightship, and thus to know exactly where they were.

Atheneum Books for Young Readers • An imprint of Simon & Schuster Children's Publishing Division • 1230 Avenue of the Americas • New York, New York 10020 • Copyright © 2007 by Brian Floca • All rights reserved, including the right of reproduction in whole or in part in any form. • Book design by Michael McCartney • The text for this book is set in Berthold Walbaum. • The illustrations for this book are rendered in watercolor and ink. • Manufactured in Mexico • First Edition • 10 9 8 7 6 5 4 3 2 1 • Library of Congress Cataloging-in-Publication Data • Floca, Brian. • Lightship / Brian Floca.–1st ed. • p.   cm. • "A Richard Jackson Book." • ISBN-13: 978-1-4169-2436-4 • ISBN-10: 1-4169-2436-1 • 1. Lightships–Juvenile literature. I. Title. • VK1013.F5 2007 • 387.2′8–dc22 • 2005028028

LIGHTSHIP

Brian Floca

A RICHARD JACKSON BOOK
ATHENEUM BOOKS FOR YOUNG READERS
NEW YORK LONDON TORONTO SYDNEY

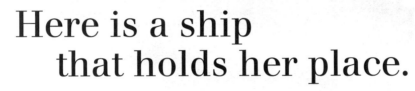

Here is a ship
that holds her place.

She has a captain and a crew:

helmsman, oiler, engineer,
deckhand, fireman, radioman,
messman, cook,

and cat.

She does not sail from port to port.

She does not carry passengers
 or mail or packages.

She holds to one sure spot
 as other ships sail by.

She waits.

Her crew lives
in small spaces,
works in small spaces.

Always there is
the salt smell of the sea . . .

and the rocking
of the waves.

Always they hear
   the creaking of the ship
   and the slow
   slap, slap, slap
   of water on the hull.

Down below the deck,
   deep inside the ship,
      there is the smell of fuel and machinery.

There are motors, engines, generators.

      The oiler and the engineer
         keep them clean and running.

      They keep the whole ship powered.

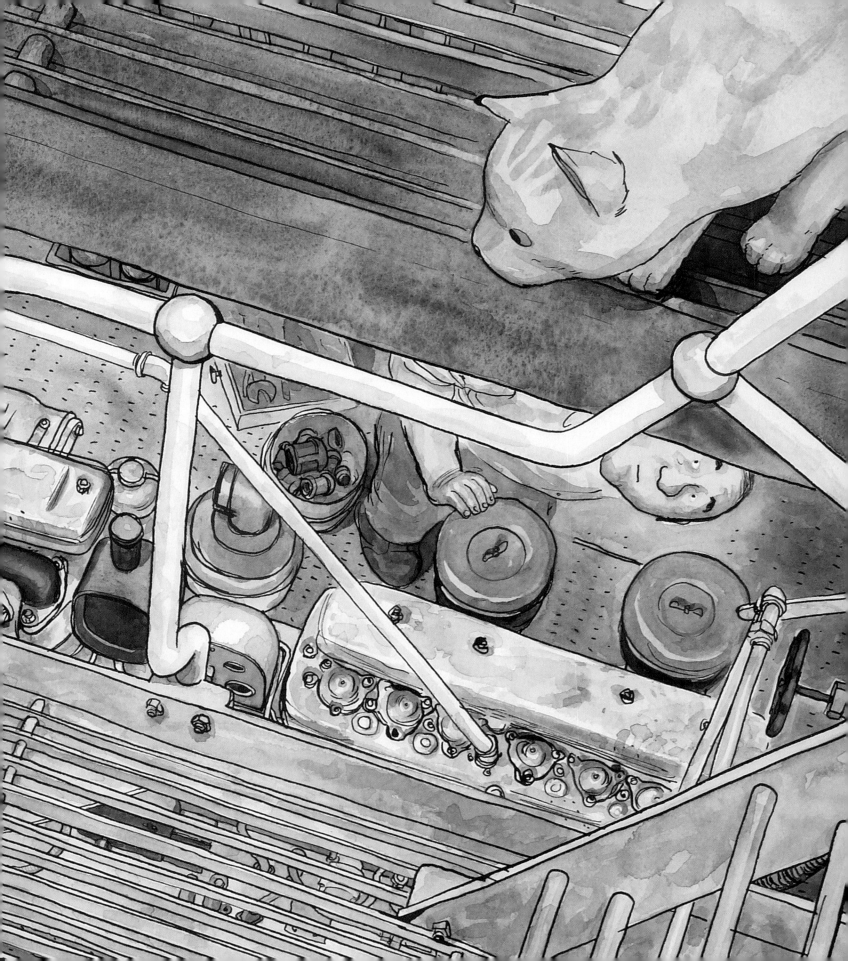

Above the deck there is a horn.
High on each mast there is a light.
The crew keeps them ready.

The higher the waves,
the harder the work;
the harder it is to climb the stairs,
to check the charts,
to drink the coffee,
to visit the head.

But the crew
keeps the lightship anchored.
She holds her one sure spot.

They keep her anchored
in sun and calm . . .

. . . and snow and cold.

They keep her anchored
when other ships
come closer
than they should.

And if the waves
move her off her mark,

. . . the helmsman moves her back.
The crew resets the anchor.

Again the lightship
holds her one sure spot.

She does not sail from port to port.

She does not carry passengers
    or mail or packages.

She holds to one sure spot
    as other ships sail by.

She waits.

And when the fog
    comes creeping in,
    the crew knows what to do.

They sound their horn
  so loud the whole ship
SHAKES.

They shine their light,
   so bright
   it reaches all around,
   far and wide.

Then other ships sail safely,
    because the lightship marks the way
    through fog and night,
    past rocks and shoals,
    past reefs and wrecks,
    past danger.

Other ships sail home safe . . .

because the lightship
holds her place.

AUTHOR'S NOTE

Lightships were floating beacons, lighthouses where lighthouses could not be built. They wore the names of the underwater hazards or shipping channels that they marked in bold letters on bright hulls, and from their single secured positions they announced themselves to other ships with lights, horns, and far-reaching radio signals. At one time lightships could be found in service across the United States. In the Pacific, the San Francisco lightship marked the entrance to the Golden Gate. The Huron and Buffalo lightships served in the Great Lakes, and the Galveston and New Orleans lightships showed the way to ports in the Gulf of Mexico. In the Atlantic, a ship marked HEN & CHICKENS warned sailors in Massachusetts' Buzzards Bay of a single large reef (the hen) in the midst of several smaller ones (the chickens). Farther east, the lightship marking the Nantucket Shoals was the first sign of America seen by ships approaching from Europe.

The idea of a lightship extends back to the ancient Romans. The English invented the modern lightship in the 1730s, and the ships came to American waters in the 1820s. Lightships operated under the authority of the Treasury Department first and then the Commerce Department, until finally being taken over by the Coast Guard in 1939. Though conditions on the ships improved vastly over the years, service on a lightship was never easy, and always had the potential to be monotonous or dangerous. Tours of duty often ran for months at a time. During stretches of foggy weather, there was the round-the-clock, bone-jarring moan of the foghorns to endure. And there was no heading to shelter when the weather grew worse than foggy. Indeed, the more hazardous the conditions on the water, the more other ships needed the point of navigation that the lightship provided. For lightship crews this meant riding out extraordinary storms on the open sea, even hurricanes strong enough to break anchor chains. Lightships were especially vulnerable to collisions because they were often positioned near shipping channels, and because other ships would sometimes set their courses by the discouraged but not uncommon practice of homing in on a lightship's radio signals. In May of 1934 the White Star liner *Olympic*, sister ship to the *Titanic*, was traveling through thick fog on a course set by the radio signals of the Nantucket lightship. Miscalculating her speed, the forty-six-thousand-ton *Olympic* overran the lightship and killed seven of her eleven-member crew.

As it became practical to build offshore towers and automated beacons, lightships were one by one retired from duty. Old ships were junked, sold to private owners, refitted for other purposes, used as target practice by the Navy, or even burned in Fourth of July celebrations (the odd fate of Light Vessel 42). A few were converted into floating exhibits, such as Light Vessel 87, which at various points in her career marked the Ambrose Channel into New York Harbor, the Scotland station off the New Jersey coast (where the wreck of the *SS Scotland* once posed a threat to other ships), and the Vineyard Sound. She is now docked at the South Street Seaport Museum in New York City, and is the ship on which the drawings for this book were based.

In 1983 the last lightship station in U.S. waters was discontinued.
After long years of service, the lightships had all sailed for port.

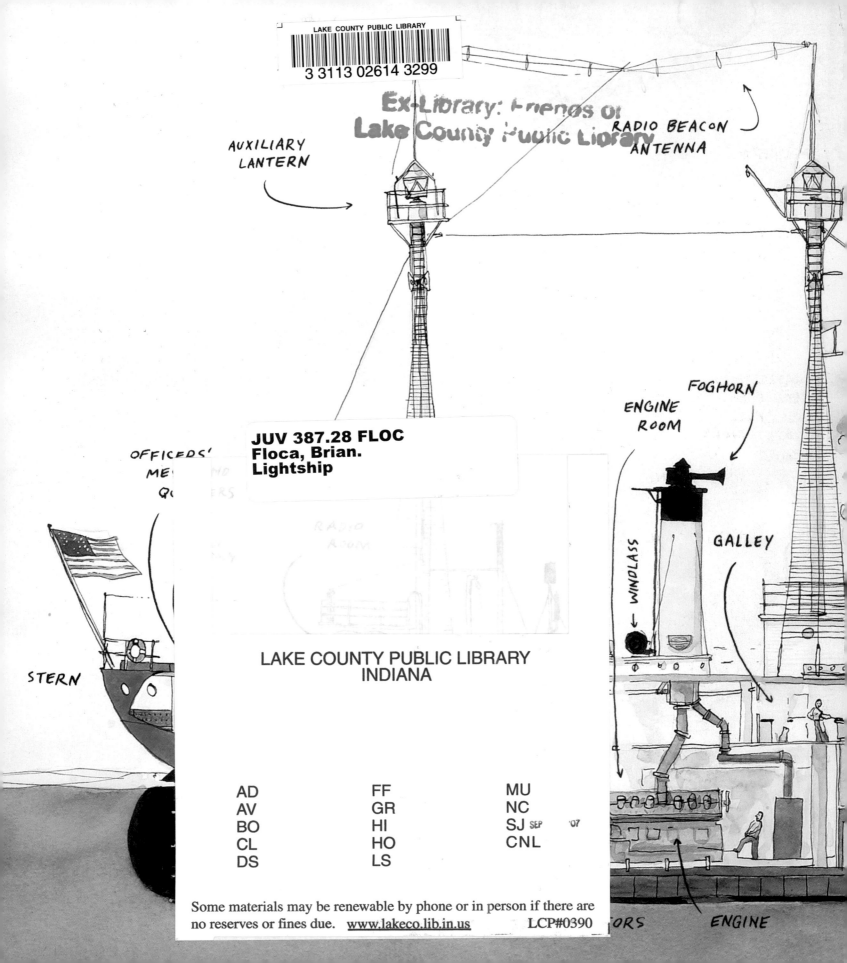

RADIO BEACON
ANTENNA

AUXILIARY
LANTERN

FOGHORN

ENGINE
ROOM

OFFICERS'
ME   AND
Q   ERS

GALLEY

WINDLASS

RADIO
ROOM

STERN

ORS

ENGINE